D1402130

THE CAMEL

BY
CARL R. GREEN
WILLIAM R. SANFORD

EDITED BY
JUDY LOCKWOOD

PUBLISHED BY
CRESTWOOD HOUSE
Mankato, MN, U.S.A.

CIP

LIBRARY OF CONGRESS CATALOGING IN PUBLICATION DATA

Green, Carl R.
  The camel

  (Wildlife, habits & habitat)
  Includes index.
  SUMMARY: Examines the physical characteristics, behavior, lifestyle and natural environment of the camel.
  1. Camels—Juvenile literature. [1. Camels.] I. Sanford, William R. (William Reynolds), 1927-   II. Lockwood, Judy.   III. Title.   IV. Series.
QL737.U54G72   1988   599.73'6—dc19   88-5957
ISBN 0-89686-385-9

International Standard Book Number:	**Library of Congress Catalog Card Number:**
0-89686-385-9	88-5957

PHOTO CREDITS: 0025-42360

Cover: Tom Stack & Associates: Gerald Corsi
Tom Stack & Associates: (Dominique Braud) 4, 11; (Adrienne T. Gibson) 7, 12, 21, 22, 27, 42-43; (Brian Parker) 14; (Fiona Sunquist) 17; (Tom Stack) 19; (Gerald Corsi) 28; (Buff Corsi) 35; (C. Benjamin) 37; (Gary Milburn) 38
DRK Photo: (Belinda Wright) 8, 25, 30, 31, 32

Produced by Carnival Enterprises.

CRESTWOOD·HOUSE

Box 3427, Mankato, MN, U.S.A. 56002

TABLE OF CONTENTS

Camels use their humps to store fat—not water—for long desert trips.

Southern California was baking in the wind blowing over the mountains from the desert. The zoo's thermometer showed 104 degrees Fahrenheit (40 degrees Centigrade). The three visitors were sweating as they stood under a giant shade tree.

"Uncle Pete, I'm hot!" Connie protested. "I didn't come to the zoo to look at ugly old camels. I want to see the elephants."

"We'll see the elephants later," Martin told her. "Uncle Pete wants to see the camels. I bet this heat makes him think he's back in the desert."

Pete Dobkins smiled at the children. They'd grown a lot during the two years he was away in Saudi Arabia. "I don't miss the desert one bit," he said, "but I would like to see the camels. The company used them to haul supplies out to the oil rig where I was working. They're not pretty animals, but they can survive heat much worse than this."

The zoo's five camels were standing in the full sun. Their big mouths moved from side to side as they chewed their cuds.

Connie wiped the sweat from her forehead. "Aren't they hot, standing there like that?" she asked.

Pete shook his head. He remembered the oil company lecture on camels. "Camels can endure the heat better than most animals," he said. "In hot weather, your body has to work hard to get rid of excess body heat. If your body temperature rises a few degrees, you feel sick. A camel doesn't have that problem. Even if its temperature goes up as much as 11 degrees Fahrenheit (6 degrees C), it still feels comfortable. When a camel does sweat, its thick, furry coat holds the cooling moisture a long time."

"Then wouldn't it be better if they sweated more?" Martin asked.

"Out on the desert, you can't waste water," Pete replied. "By not sweating much, the camel conserves the water in its body."

Connie thought of something a friend had told her. "I've heard that camels can go for days and days without taking a drink," she said. "Is that because they don't sweat?"

"That's part of it," Pete agreed. "Camels also make good use of the water content in the plants they eat. Some desert grasses and shrubs are 50 percent water! They also get water from the early morning dew that forms on the plants. I've heard of camels going for three months without taking a drink of water!"

Martin was looking at the camels' high, rounded humps. "I know about that," he said proudly. "The camels store water in their humps! That way, it's there when they need it."

"I'm sorry, Martin, but it doesn't work that way," Pete said. "The hump doesn't hold water. It's filled with about 100 pounds (45 kilograms) of fat. The fat

A camel's whole body has adapted to the desert's dry conditions.

is the camel's reserve food supply. When the camel can't find plants to eat, its body uses the fat for energy. Camel drivers check the condition of their animals by looking at their humps. If the hump is high and solid, the camel is ready for a trip across the desert. The hump of a starving camel looks like a balloon with the air let out."

"Why do the humps look so solid if they're full of fat?" Connie wondered.

"The layers of fat are held together by tough body tissue," Pete said. "The hump is solid enough to hold a saddle and rider."

"Okay," Martin put in, "but where's the rest of their fat? Except for the humps, those camels look all skin and bones."

"There's a reason for that, too," Pete said. "It's too hot in the desert to wear a blanket of fat all over the body. Camels store most of their fat in their humps. Their thick, wooly coats keep them warm on cold nights. Any way you look at it, camels are built for survival."

Pete looked at his watch. "It's getting late," he said. "We'll move on if you want to see the elephants."

"That's okay," Connie said. "Let's stay and learn more about camels. You were right. They're not pretty, but they are interesting."

Camels can be ill-tempered and smelly!

CHAPTER ONE:

Most people think of camels as desert animals from the faraway Middle East. They're surprised to learn that these large, plant-eating mammals first developed in North America. Forty million years ago, camels were rabbit-sized and lacked humps. In time, the camels developed into a number of species, one of which stood over ten feet (3 meters) tall. They all belong to a family naturalists call the *camelidae* (or *camelids*).

The camelids spread out in all directions. One branch of the family migrated to South America. Today's llamas and alpacas are descended from these early camelids. Another type of camelid wandered north during the ice age and crossed a land bridge between Alaska and Asia. Later, when the glaciers melted, the bridge vanished under the waters of the Bering Strait. The camel died out in North America, but adapted well to its new home in central Asia.

Domesticating animals

About 125,000 years ago, early humans made a great leap forward. Until that time, Stone Age people had lived by hunting and gathering. Then people began to capture and tame animals. Experts call this the process of domestication. Domestic animals not only carried loads, they also provided humans with a stable food supply. Human progress came faster after that.

Most of the wild animals that have been domesticated seem to have developed a liking for their masters. That has never been true of the camel. Today's camels are just as stubborn and ill-tempered as their ancestors. Camel drivers say that their animals are lazy, mean, and stupid. If a camel thinks its load is too heavy, it refuses to stand up! As often as not, it will spit on anyone who walks too close.

Despite these drawbacks, camels were marvelous beasts of burden. In about 2,600 B.C., the nomadic people of central Iran captured and tamed the wild camels of the region. These were the two-humped animals called *bactrians*. Bactrians carried heavy loads across the freezing mountain passes of Turkestan, northern India, and China. The camels also provided meat, milk, and wool. Even their dung was used — it was dried and burned as fuel.

The one-humped camel developed further south. Today, it is often called the Arabian camel because of its long history of use in that part of the world. Arabian camels have longer legs and carry heavier loads than their bactrian cousins. They are well suited to hot, dry lands, for they can go without water for days at a time. Just as important, Arabian camels eat

The bactrian camel was first tamed in 2,600 B.C.

desert plants that sheep and horses won't touch. In time, one-humped camels spread from the Middle East to North Africa, East Africa, and India.

Dromedaries carry people rather than heavy loads.

Camels haven't changed much

As humans domesticate a species, they change the animal to fit their needs. This is usually done by breeding only those animals that have the qualities people want. The camel is an exception to this rule. After 4,000 years, the modern camel looks much like the ancient camel.

The closest to a new breed is the riding camel, sometimes called the dromedary. Dromedaries are bred for speed and endurance rather than for carrying heavy loads. They carry their riders across desert sands at surprising speeds. In 15 hours, a dromedary can cover 90 miles (144 kilometers) or more!

Wild camels are almost extinct

Are there any wild camels left today? Wildlife experts aren't certain. Camel herds wander free in the Gobi Desert of Mongolia and in the outback of Australia. The argument centers on whether these camels are wild or feral. A truly wild animal has never been domesticated. A feral animal, by contrast, is a domestic animal that has returned to the wild.

The Australian camels are clearly feral. They were imported to Australia in the 1800s for use as pack

A camel's hoofs are really large toenails.

animals. When machines replaced them, some of the camels were released and returned to a wild state. The Gobi bactrians, however, seem to be truly wild. They are slender camels with smaller humps than domestic bactrians. Their feet are smaller, and their hair is shorter. Wild or feral, the Gobi camels may soon be extinct. Fewer than 1,000 are left alive to roam their high, lonely habitat.

CHAPTER TWO:

Camels belong to a large group of animals called the *artiodactyla*. All artiodactyls are hoofed mammals with an even number of toes on each foot. Other artiodactyls are cattle, deer, and the hippopotamus. Among these animals, the two-toed camel was one of the first to appear.

Unlike the other artiodactyls, a camel walks on a sole-pad, not on a hoof. Its "hoofs" are really large, heavy toenails. The toenails touch the ground, but the camel's weight is supported by thick, elastic sole-pads. This pad is as much as seven inches (18 centimeters) wide. It keeps the camel from sinking into soft sand and drifting snow.

Calluses on knees and chest

As well as being an artiodactyl, camels belong to the suborder *tylopoda*. In Greek, "tylopoda" means "callous feet." This name refers to the hard, thick calluses that protect the camel's knees and chest. These are the parts of the body that rub on the ground when the camel kneels. Camels are also unusual in another way. Their legs are joined to the body in a way that allows them to rest on their knees with legs tucked underneath.

When a camel kneels, it first bends its front legs until it's kneeling. Then it folds its hind legs and drops heavily to the ground. The calluses protect the knee joints and the breastbone. In order to stand up, the camel reverses the process. It rises on its front knees. Then it pushes upward with its rear legs until they're straight. Finally it stands upright, one front leg at a time. The process isn't graceful, but it gets the job done!

Large and brown

Bactrian camels are adapted to cold, dry habitats, while Arabian camels live in hot, dry places. At a quick glance, the only difference between the two is the number of humps. A more careful check would show that bactrians have heavier bones, shorter legs, and thicker coats. Otherwise, the two camels are very much alike. Arabian camels, in fact, do have a second hump. It's so small, though, that it's nearly invisible.

A full-grown bactrian camel stands seven feet (2 m) at the hump. An average Arabian camel is about six inches (15 cm) shorter. Both animals are about ten feet (3 m) long, from nose to rump. The rope-like tail ends in a tuft of hair, and adds another 18 inches (46 cm). Both species average about 1,200 pounds (545 kg) in weight. Females are smaller and lighter.

Bactrian camels have thicker coats than Arabian camels.

A camel's thick coat of short, wooly hair protects it from both cold and heat. Most Arabian camels are light brown, but white, grey, reddish-brown, and black camels are fairly common. A few are spotted. When used in clothing, the Arabian's tan color is commonly known as "camel." The thick coat helps keep the camel cool by holding sweat so that it evaporates slowly. Bactrian camels tend to be dark brown. Their coats grow as long as ten inches (25 cm) in the winter.

All camels shed their hair, a process called molting.

In the spring, the old fur falls out in untidy clumps that stick to the animal's body. When the molt is finally over, the camels look sleek and clean. The new coat grows in almost at once.

A mouth tough enough to chew thorns

Camels are plant eaters with sharp, strong teeth. A newborn camel has three pairs of incisors (cutting teeth) in each jaw. As it matures, it loses the four middle incisors from the upper jaw. A hard, bony ridge grows in the empty space. Camels also have four canines (tearing teeth) and 22 molars and premolars (grinding teeth).

A camel uses its lips to pull up grass, strip leaves, or break twigs off shrubs. It chops off each mouthful by biting against the bony ridge in its upper jaw. With a tough tongue and mouth, the camel munches happily on plants with thorns as long as four inches (10 cm). The upper lip is split so that the camel can bite off plants close to the ground. When angry, the camel curls its upper lip and spits with great accuracy.

As the camel ages, its teeth turn yellow, and its breath gets bad. Only people with strong stomachs look at them closely!

Camels use their split upper lip to eat plants that grow close to the ground.

Senses adapted to its habitat

A camel has well-developed senses. As with other plant eaters, a camel's eyes are located on the sides of its head. This allows the camel to see in all directions. Since it grazes at night, it sees almost as well in dim light as during the day. The upper and lower eyelids are thin enough to let in some light. This allows a camel to find its way through a blinding sandstorm with its eyes tightly closed!

Heavy eyebrows above each eye provide shade from the bright desert sun. In addition, long, curly eyelashes screen out blowing sand or freezing snow. If any sand gets through, a third eyelid wipes it away before it gets into the eye.

The camel's sense of smell works equally well. If people are lost in the desert, their camels sometimes lead them to an oasis. The animals can detect the faint scent of water from miles away. Special muscles close off the nostrils to keep out blowing sand or sleet.

The ears are similarly protected by a thick growth of hair. Camels have good ears, but they hear only what they want to hear. They often pretend not to hear orders from their riders!

A ruminant with three stomachs

Like other artiodactyls, camels are *ruminants*— plant eaters with multi-chambered stomachs that chew a cud. Most ruminants have four chambers in their stomachs, but camels have only three. This probably is because camels were the first ruminants to develop.

When it's feeding, a camel swallows its food almost whole. The food mass is stored in the rumen, or first stomach. In the rumen, bacteria begin the breakdown

Even in the middle of the desert, camels can detect water.

of the tough plant fibers. Later at a quiet time, the camel coughs up a ball of this material (the cud). After chewing its cud for a while, the camel swallows it again. This time, the well-chewed pulp goes on to the second and third stomachs. These chambers complete the process of digestion and release the food energy.

The camel's body also makes good use of water; it can go many days without a drink. The water content of plants is enough to satisfy the camel's needs. In a pinch, a camel can lose 40 percent of its body moisture and remain healthy. Most mammals die if they lose half that much. The length of time a camel can go without water is hard to figure. The answer depends on many things—diet, sun, wind, and work load.

These adaptations to desert living give the camel an average life span of 25 years. Some live as long as 40 years. This long life is surprising, for the camel occupies a harsh and nearly waterless habitat.

Camels will eat almost anything—even thorny bushes.

CHAPTER THREE:

The blinding sun scorches the desert sand. A slight breeze stirs the leaves of palm trees near a small oasis. The moving air seems to sear the skin. Humans lost in these wastes are blistered by sun and sand. Sweat flows freely as their bodies try to cope with temperatures well above 100 degrees Fahrenheit (38 degrees C).

Adapted to both heat and cold

At first, the desert looks empty of life. As far as one can see, the land seems almost as barren as the surface of the moon. Then in the distance, tall brown shadows appear. A herd of Arabian camels is grazing on thorn bushes. The sun and heat don't seem to bother them. Throughout India, the Middle East, and North Africa, Arabian camels occupy desert habitats.

In the high deserts and mountain passes of central Asia, summer gives way to winter. Freezing winds knife through the thickest clothing. Bactrian camels ignore the wind as they plod over icy trails. These two-humped camels endure cold weather as easily as they do the summer heat. Shorter and bulkier than Arabian camels, the bactrians are better at saving their body heat. Long coats keep out the frost, and their large sole-pads act like snowshoes. If food is hard to find, they live on the fat stored in their humps.

Control of body temperature

The body shape that makes the camel look like a cartoon animal is perfect for the desert. The long legs lift the camel high above the hot sand, so that moving air can cool its belly. The animal's behavior also has adapted to the heat. When camels graze, they face the sun. This exposes the smallest area of their bodies to the warming rays. In cool weather, they stand with their sides turned to the sun for maximum warmth.

The camel adjusts its body temperature to desert conditions. At sunrise, a camel may have a temperature as low as 93 degrees Fahrenheit (34 degrees C). In the heat of the day, its temperature may rise to 104 degrees Fahrenheit (40 degrees C). At night, the camel slowly releases this stored heat to guard against the cold.

Making do with little water

Camels make excellent use of the water they drink. If their food has enough moisture in it, they can survive on that. In hot weather, working camels drink three to five gallons (11 to 19 liters) of water every other day. A camel that has gone without water for many days uses up its body fluids. Given the chance to drink, it will gulp down 30 gallons (114 liters) of water in a few minutes—which is about three buckets!

Making good use of water isn't the same as storing it. The camel doesn't store water in its stomach, and the hump is a storehouse for fat, not water. Water can be recovered from fat, but scientists calculate that the energy cost would be too great. The camel would lose more water than it would gain.

When water is available, camels can drink 30 gallons at one time!

Camels will eat almost anything

Camels love to eat, and they'll eat almost anything. A camel kept in a zoo consumes about eight pounds (4 kg) of food each day. Work camels, however, need up to 44 pounds (20 kg) of grass, leaves, and twigs. Turned loose at night while their owners sleep, they usually find enough food to keep them well fed. With their front legs loosely chained, they won't wander too far. If they do, the lure of water and salt will bring them back.

Out on the desert camels move from plant to plant, nibbling as they go. They take only one or two bites from each patch of grass or shrub. This type of grazing makes plants grow faster instead of destroying them. Left to themselves, camels will graze for eight to twelve hours a day. Their favorite snacks are cram-cram grass, thornbushes, acacia trees, and saltbushes. They will eat anything, from oats and hay to fish and leather harnesses!

Tireless "ships of the desert"

Pack camels travel at a pace of about three miles (5 km) per hour. Each camel carries a load of 500 pounds (226 kg) for a day's journey of 25 miles (40

After a day of traveling, pack camels are unloaded and allowed to graze freely.

km). Dromedaries average five miles (8 km) per hour for long distances. Racing dromedaries can be prodded into a faster gallop, but not for long.

As it walks, a camel swings both left legs forward and then both right legs forward, like a pacing horse. Its head bobs up and down and its body sways from side to side. When people call camels the "ships of the desert," they may be thinking of this rocking motion. New riders often complain of feeling seasick, but experts say that a camel actually gives a very smooth ride.

Sometimes a whip is needed to discipline domestic camels.

Fighting and mating

Male camels can be highly aggressive during the mating season. That's why North African camel breeders kill or geld most male calves at birth (geldings are incapable of fathering offspring). In wild and feral herds, the strongest males gather a harem of several females. Bachelor males form their own herds and fight the harem males for mates. In herds of domestic camels, the males must battle for the attention of the females. They roar, kick, bite, and try to wrestle each other to the ground. The goal is to crush the opponent by falling on him. If the owners see this, they use whips to break up the fights.

The winners stalk around the females, hoping to gain their favor. A dark, smelly liquid flows from poll glands located at the back of their heads. The males bend down and rub the greasy liquid on trees and bushes to mark their territory. As they approach the females, they make a gurgling noise. Arabian males also inflate their soft palates (the roofs of their mouths). They look as if they're blowing big, pink bubbles.

Large, fast-growing calves

Female camels breed every two years, starting at the age of four or five. The female carries her calf for 12 to 13 months before giving birth. Most births produce only a single calf. A newborn calf weighs about 80 pounds (36 kg) and stands four feet (1.2 m) high at the hump.

A calf is born with its eyes open and stands on long, shaky legs within an hour or two. The newborn camel bleats like a sheep to tell its mother that it's hungry. As soon as it can stand upright, the calf begins to

A newborn calf receives careful attention from its mother.

nurse. Camels are one of the few animals that don't clean their newborns by licking them.

Most calves are born during the desert's brief wet season. A diet of fresh green plants helps the females produce milk. A calf nurses for only three or four months. Although it's weaned early, the young camel stays with its mother for four years. A female won't allow herself to be separated from her calf. When she decides that it's time for the four-year-old to be on its own, she turns away and ignores it. If the young camel follows her, the female turns and gives it a hard kick.

Long, shakey legs support a calf soon after birth.

CHAPTER FOUR:

Camels are stubborn, ill-tempered, and smelly. They bite and spit and lay down on the job. Despite all this, they're one of the most useful of all domesticated animals. Arabian and bactrian camels

Herdsmen in India use camels to carry supplies across the desert.

are excellent pack animals that can be hitched to wagons or plows. Dromedaries carry their riders across barren lands where roads don't exist. But camels are useful in many other ways, too.

Many people depend on the camel for food. The meat of a young camel tastes much like veal. People in the Middle East eat sliced camel meat flavored with garlic. Camel milk, too, is useful. The creamy milk makes rich butter and cheese.

People also gather the wool shed by the camel during its molt. For centuries, the wool has been woven into warm blankets. The longer and thicker bactrian wool is thought to be the best of all. Most clothing stores carry expensive overcoats and sport jackets made of camel hair. Even the camel's tough skin is useful. Tanned hides make good saddles, water bags, and sandals.

Useful in peace and in war

For thousands of years, people in Asia, North Africa, and the Middle East listened for the sound of camel bells. The bells meant that a caravan was coming. The caravan's merchants traveled together for safety. Their camels carried silks, rugs, incense, and spices from the Orient. The merchants traded their goods for gold, amber, ivory, and furs from Africa and Europe.

Camels have long been used in war as well as in peace. The Babylonians began using war camels about 2,400 B.C. The sight of armed men mounted on camels terrorized soldiers on foot. Men riding horses could move faster than men on camels, but the camels had one great advantage. When they retreated into the desert, the horses could not follow them. One Indian emperor commanded a camel cavalry of 12,000 warriors. As late as the 1800s, the British and French armies kept camel corps in North Africa.

Definitely not perfect

If the camel is so useful, why did people wait so long to domesticate it? To put it simply, camels are hard to train. They have bad tempers, they learn slowly — and they smell bad! Humans can endure the smell, but horses go out of control when they smell camels. An early historian tells how camels won a battle for Persia's Cyrus the Great against Lydia. When Cyrus saw the strength of the Lydian horsemen, he gathered all of his camels together. Then he sent the camels and their riders against the Lydian cavalry. The Lydian warhorses caught the strong smell of camels and bolted from the battlefield. Cyrus won an easy victory.

Camels and farming don't mix well, either. Farmers need plenty of water for their crops. But what's good for wheat and cotton is bad for camels. In moist or humid weather, camels fall prey to many diseases.

Camels are hard to train and are known for their bad tempers.

They're also expensive to feed unless they can be turned loose to graze. Where farms are small and land is precious, there isn't enough grazing land for camels.

How do you saddle a camel?

Loading a camel is different than loading most pack animals. Camels are so tall they have to lie down to be loaded. Even when they're behaving, camels moan and grumble. If the drivers aren't careful, they'll get a nasty bite or a big glob of spit. At other times, the camels lie down instead of kneeling. When the camels misbehave this way, drivers do lots of shouting and tugging on the ropes tied to the animals' lower jaws.

Inventing a saddle to fit a camel's hump wasn't easy. Over the years, two basic camel saddles were designed. One type fastens in front of the hump. This allows the rider's weight to rest on the camel's shoulders. The more common saddle has a padded frame that fits around the hump. The rider sits in a soft leather saddle that rests on top of the frame. This spreads the weight evenly over the camel's ribcage.

When carrying cargo, the driver balances the load and ties it to the frame. Older camels know exactly how heavy their loads should be. If they don't like the weight or the balance, they won't stand up. Kicks and tugs and shouts don't do any good. The camels won't budge until the load is reduced or repacked.

A soft, leather cushion makes an excellent camel saddle.

Camels in art and religion

Ancient peoples made the camel a part of their arts and their religions. Images of camels were made in clay, bronze, copper, silver, and gold. Camels were carved on the tombs of Assyrian, Egyptian, and Chinese rulers. Many Middle Eastern religions believed that a sacrifice of camels was pleasing to their gods. Not everyone agreed. Jews and early

Christians thought the camel was unclean. In Persia, Moslems believed the places where camels rested were visited by devils.

Today, beliefs and stories about the camel still show up in many cultures. In Arabic-speaking countries, villagers don't use their children's names when calling for them. They shout, "Jamal" (which means camel). This is meant to confuse evil spirits, who must know a person's name before they can do harm. Many children around the world know the story of the camel that wanted to come in out of the cold. The kindly owner allowed the beast to put its nose into the tent.

In the 1840s, camels were used to carry supplies in the United States.

Little by little, the camel inched forward. Soon it had its head and neck inside. The owner protested, but the camel pretended not to hear. Before long, the camel had its whole body inside the tent—and the owner was pushed outside!

Children in North America might say, "That's interesting, but the only camels on this continent are in zoos." They wouldn't say that if they knew the story of Uncle Sam's Camel Corps. Believe it or not, camels helped open the American West.

CHAPTER FIVE:

Most people think of horses, cattle, and buffalo when they think of the Old West. Camels played a role in opening up the desert lands of the United States, too. Their story begins in 1848. That was when victory in the Mexican War added over 500,000 square miles (1,295,000 sq. km) to the western U.S.

Travel was dangerous and costly

The trip westward across this vast territory was long and dangerous. That didn't stop settlers from heading west by wagon train. The settlers weren't the only ones interested in the west. The U.S. Army set up forts to protect their new territory.

The forts needed a constant stream of supplies. The run from San Diego, California, to Fort Yuma, Arizona, was 180 miles (288 km). Every ton (907 kg) of freight hauled over that trail cost at least $500. This was a huge sum of money in the 1850s.

Camel Corps!

In 1855, the U.S. Congress voted to set up a U.S. Camel Corps. If the plan worked, the camels would cut the cost of carrying freight to the western forts. A U.S. ship sailed to North Africa and Asia to buy the camels. In the Crimea, near the Black Sea, U.S. officers saw camels being used in war. They were amazed to see soldiers, riding two to a camel, cover 70 miles (112 km) in 12 hours.

The first camels arrived at Indianola, Texas, in 1856. The camel drivers led 76 camels into a corral made of prickly pear cactus. The hungry camels quickly made a meal of the cactus! Twenty-eight of the camels were shipped on to California the following year.

No love at first sight

The camels were not wildly popular. Soldiers preferred horses and mules. They didn't like the bad-tempered camels, and loading them was difficult. Some camels developed sores on their backs from badly-loaded packs. Worse yet, the camels frightened other animals. Horses reared and galloped away when camels came near. Brownsville, Texas, passed a law making it illegal to bring camels into town.

Despite the problems, the Camel Corps proved its worth. Loaded with over 1,200 pounds (544 kg) of hay, one camel easily stood up and walked off with its cargo. Trips to San Antonio proved that six camels could carry as much freight as 12 horses in half the time. The camels slogged through sand and climbed mountain trails that no horse-drawn wagon could handle.

A meal of "camel clover"

The camels liked their new habitat. Even though they carried water for horses, they seldom needed a drink for themselves. Instead, they wolfed down sagebrush, mesquite, prickly pear, and other thorny

Camels are unusual — but useful — animals.

plants. The soldiers marveled at their appetites and said that the beasts were eating "camel clover."

The experiment ended when the Civil War began. The southern states were too busy fighting to worry about camels. A few carried mail along the Texas-Mexico border, but others were turned loose. Three wandered off and were captured in Arkansas by Union Soldiers. By the end of the war, all interest in the Camel Corps had faded.

Feral camels and ghost stories

Some of the remaining camels were released in Arizona. The camels quickly turned feral. By 1870, they had spread as far as Nevada. All through the 1800s, travelers were amazed to see camels roaming free on the desert. Small herds ranged from Texas to New Mexico, Arizona, and California's Death Valley. As late as 1941, a lone camel was seen on the shores of California's Salton Sea. Perhaps that was the last survivor of the Camel Corps.

The camels are gone now, but they're not forgotten. Tall tales, told around campfires, remind us of the days when camels lived in the American West. One tale describes a camel that still crosses the desert at night. The ghostly camel is carrying a human skeleton on its back.

MAP:

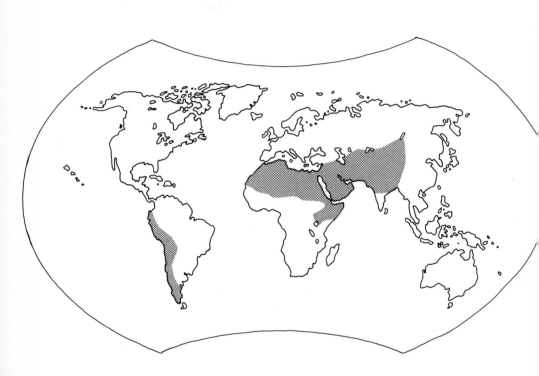

Most camels live within these areas.

INDEX/GLOSSARY:

WILDLIFE
HABITS & HABITAT

READ AND ENJOY THE SERIES:

If you would like to know more about all kinds of wildlife, you should take a look at the other books in this series.

You'll find books on bald eagles and other birds. Books on alligators and other reptiles. There are books about deer and other big-game animals. And there are books about sharks and other creatures that live in the ocean.

In all of the books you will learn that life in the wild is not easy. But you will also learn what people can do to help wildlife survive. So read on!